ALICE GUSTAFSON
SCHOOL
LEARNING CENTER

DATE DUE			

My First NFL Book

NEW ENGLAND PATRIOTS

Nate Cohn

LET'S READ
AV2 BY WEIGL
ADDED VALUE · AUDIO VISUAL

www.av2books.com

LET'S READ
AV²
BY WEIGL™
ADDED VALUE • AUDIO VISUAL

Go to **www.av2books.com**, and enter this book's unique code.

BOOK CODE

Y895855

AV² by Weigl brings you media enhanced books that support active learning.

AV² provides enriched content that supplements and complements this book. Weigl's AV² books strive to create inspired learning and engage young minds in a total learning experience.

Your AV² Media Enhanced books come alive with...

Audio
Listen to sections of the book read aloud.

Video
Watch informative video clips.

Embedded Weblinks
Gain additional information for research.

Try This!
Complete activities and hands-on experiments.

Key Words
Study vocabulary, and complete a matching word activity.

Quizzes
Test your knowledge.

Slide Show
View images and captions, and prepare a presentation.

... and much, much more!

Published by AV² by Weigl
350 5th Avenue, 59th Floor
New York, NY 10118

Website: www.av2books.com

Printed in the United States of America in Brainerd, Minnesota
1 2 3 4 5 6 7 8 9 0 21 20 19 18 17

032017
020317

Editor: Katie Gillespie
Art Director: Terry Paulhus

Weigl acknowledges Getty Images and iStock as the primary image suppliers for this title.

Library of Congress Control Number: 2017930773

ISBN 978-1-4896-5526-4 (hardcover)
ISBN 978-1-4896-5528-8 (multi-user eBook)

My First NFL Book

NEW ENGLAND PATRIOTS

CONTENTS

Team History

The New England Patriots started playing football in 1960. They are the only NFL team that plays for a region rather than one or two states. The team plays for New England. This includes Connecticut, Maine, Massachusetts, New Hampshire, Rhode Island, and Vermont.

The 2016 Patriots were the first NFL team to win a Super Bowl in overtime.

The Stadium

The Patriots play in Gillette Stadium. The stadium has a 12-story lighthouse. This is because New England is known for its lighthouses. There is also a bridge. It looks like one of the bridges in the nearby city of Boston.

Gillette Stadium is in Foxborough, Massachusetts. It is farther east than any other NFL field.

Team Spirit

A patriot is someone who defends his or her country. Pat Patriot is the team's mascot. He wears a hat like those worn by U.S. soldiers in the American Revolutionary War. He dresses in red, white, and blue. Those are the team colors. They are also the colors of the United States.

A cartoonist at a Boston newspaper made up the Pat Patriot character.

The Jerseys

The team's first jerseys were red for home games and white for away games. The Patriots switched to bright blue shirts for home games in the 1990s. Players now wear jerseys that are a dark navy blue with red and silver trim for most of their home games.

The Helmet

The Patriots' first helmets were white. Today's helmets are silver with a red facemask. The logo on the helmets is called the Flying Elvis. This is because some people think it looks like Elvis Presley. He was a singer who became famous in the 1950s.

The first Patriots logo showed a hat from the American Revolutionary War.

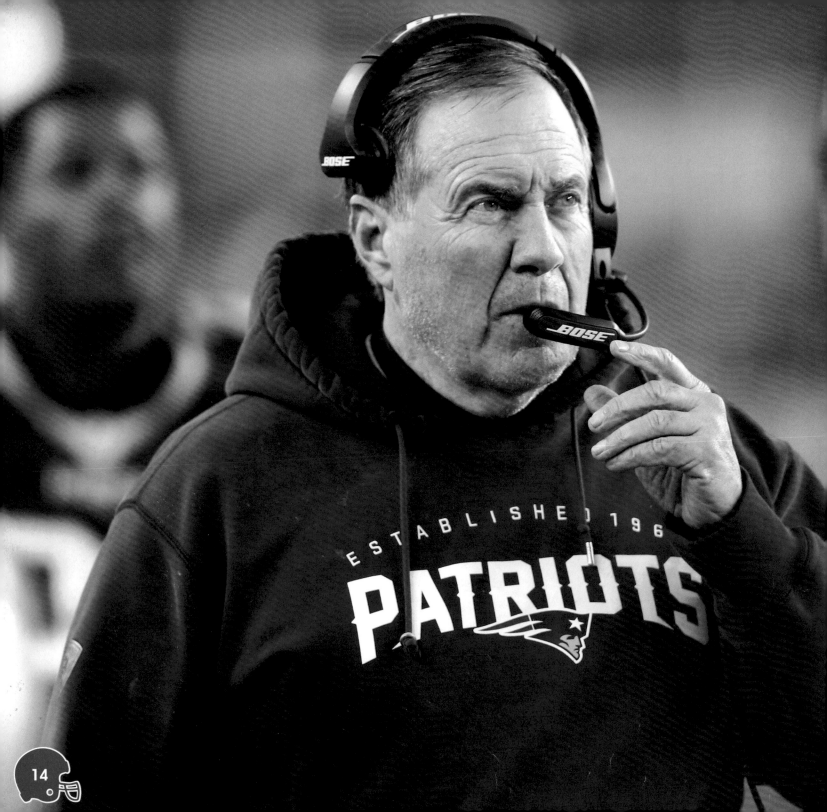

The Coach

Bill Belichick is the head coach of the Patriots. He is known for wearing a sweatshirt during games. He is also known for winning. The NFL is split into eight divisions. Belichick led the Patriots to 14 division titles from 2001 to 2016. He coached the team in seven Super Bowls and won five of them.

Player Positions

Slot receivers are wide receivers who start close to the offensive line. Being in this position makes it easier to catch quick passes. Some slot receivers are big and strong. They try to break free from any contact. Others try to escape from the defenders.

Many people think that slot receivers are the most important offensive players.

Tom Brady is the Patriots' quarterback. Brady has been named the Super Bowl's Most Valuable Player four times. He has won five Super Bowls. This is a record for NFL quarterbacks. Brady reached 208 total wins in 2016. This made him the quarterback with the most wins ever in NFL history.

18

Andre Tippett was a linebacker for the Patriots for 12 seasons. He made 100 sacks for the team. A sack is when a defensive player tackles the quarterback before the ball can be passed. Tippett was named Defensive Player of the Year in 1985. He is in the Pro Football Hall of Fame.

Famous Player

Team Records

The 32 NFL teams are divided into two conferences. Conference winners play each other every year. The Patriots have won nine conference titles. Running back Kevin Faulk moved the ball 12,349 yards in his career. This is a team record. The 2007 team was undefeated in the 16-game regular season.

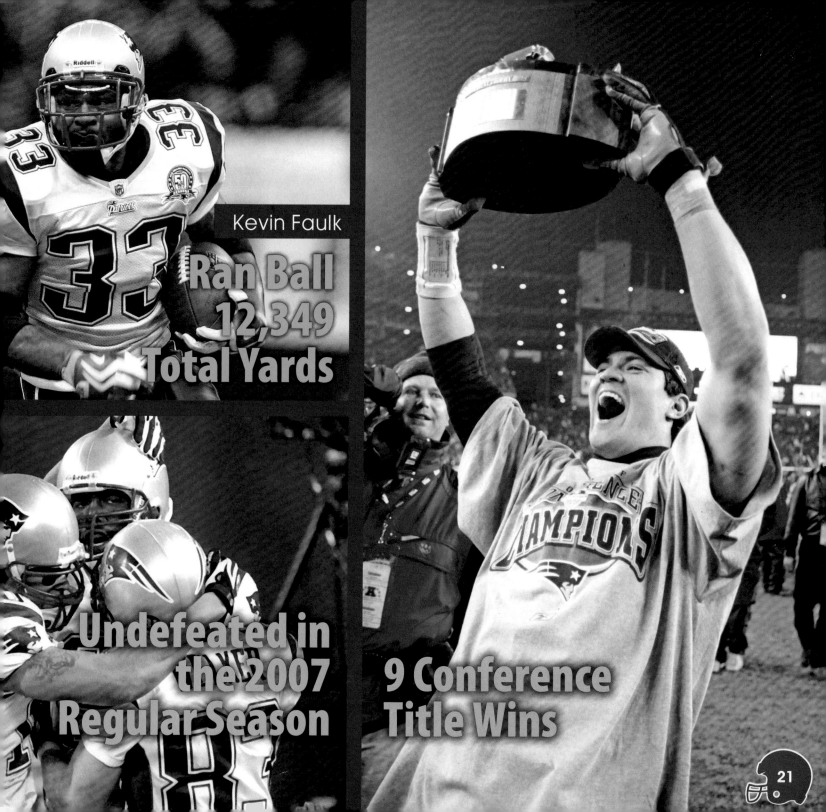

Kevin Faulk

Ran Ball
12,349
Total Yards

Undefeated in
the 2007
Regular Season

9 Conference
Title Wins

21

By the Numbers

The Patriots have played in **9 Super Bowls.** This is the most of any NFL team ever.

Bill Belichick was named NFL Coach of the Year **3 times.**

Running back LeGarrette Blount was the NFL's 2016 rushing touchdown **leader.** He scored **18 times.**

Gillette Stadium has an area of **1.9 million** square feet.

Tom Brady has started in

7 Super Bowls.

This is more than any other NFL quarterback.

Tight end Rob Gronkowski's height is

6 feet 6 inches.

Quiz

1. In what year did the Patriots start playing football?

2. Where is Gillette Stadium?

3. What is Bill Belichick known for wearing during games?

4. What are wide receivers who start close to the offensive line called?

5. How many sacks did Andre Tippett make for the Patriots?

Check out www.av2books.com for activities, videos, audio clips, and more!

1 Go to www.av2books.com.

2 Enter book code. **Y 8 9 5 8 5 5**

3 Fuel your imagination online!

www.av2books.com